FORMATTING LETTERS AND REPORTS
A Computer User's Guide

Eleanor Davidson, Ph.D.

A FIFTY-MINUTE™ SERIES BOOK

CRISP PUBLICATIONS, INC.
Menlo Park, California

FORMATTING LETTERS AND REPORTS
A Computer User's Guide

Eleanor Davidson, Ph.D.

CREDITS:
Editor: **Bev Manber**
Designer: **Carol Harris**
Typesetting: **ExecuStaff**
Cover Design: **Kathleen Gadway**
Artwork: **Ralph Mapson**

Copyright © 1992 Crisp Publications, Inc.
Printed in the United States of America by Bawden Printing Company.

English language Crisp books are distributed worldwide. Our major international distributors include:

CANADA: Reid Publishing, Ltd., Box 69559—109 Thomas St., Oakville, Ontario Canada L6J 7R4. TEL: (416) 842-4428; FAX: (416) 842-9327

AUSTRALIA: Career Builders, P.O. Box 1051, Springwood, Brisbane, Queensland, Australia 4127. TEL: 841-1061, FAX: 841-1580

NEW ZEALAND: Career Builders, P.O. Box 571, Manurewa, Auckland, New Zealand. TEL: 266-5276, FAX: 266-4152

JAPAN: Phoenix Associates Co., Mizuho Bldg. 2-12-2, Kami Osaki, Shinagawa-Ku, Tokyo 141, Japan. TEL: 3-443-7231, FAX: 3-443-7640

Selected Crisp titles are also available in other languages. Contact International Rights Manager Suzanne Kelly at (415) 323-6100 for more information.

Library of Congress Catalog Card Number 91-76XXX
Davidson, Eleanor
The Computer User's Guide
ISBN 1-56052-130-9

This book is printed on recyclable paper with soy ink.

PREFACE

In many ways, computers have made our jobs easier. They have also created increased expectations about the quality and amount of work we can accomplish. This book is written for anyone who types letters and reports on a computer and wants them to look as professional as possible. This easy-to-read guide addresses many of the everyday questions you may have been asking, but have not known where to find answers.

Your job will be made simpler by following the basic guidelines contained in this book. You will find answers to questions such as:

- What is the correct way to address a letter?
- What are the required parts of a letter?
- When should I use a colon, comma, parenthesis, the dash?
- How many spaces should I leave and under what circumstances?
- How do I type an envelope?
- What is the correct way to prepare a Title Page?
- What is the difference between a footnote and an endnote, and how do I type them?
- How do I keyboard quotations?
- What are rules for capitalization, abbreviations, typing numbers and dividing words?

At the end of the book are some useful writing tips and reference lists, including Computer Terminology, State Abbreviations and Proofreader's Marks.

You can read through the book now, or just familiarize yourself with its contents. Then, keep it on your shelf, within reach, for those critical times when you are baffled by questions about formatting letters and reports. Your work will be easier, and you will get more accomplished with less frustration. And, your letters and reports will look more impressive, so the recipients will be more likely to take what you write seriously!

Good luck!

CONTENTS

INTRODUCTION 1

PART I   LETTERS 3

   Appearance of the Letter 5
   Your Word Processing Software 6
   Letter Placement Guide 7
   Required Parts of a Letter 10
   Letter Styles 13
   Block Style Letter 14
   Modified Block Style Letter 16
   Simplified Letter 18
   Optional Parts of a Letter 20
   Envelopes 24

PART II   REPORTS 27

   Report Format and Word Processing Software 29
   Your Word Processing Software 30
   Format for Reports 31
   Documenting Sources Used in Preparing Your Report 34
   Additional Parts of a Report 38

PART III   WRITING TIPS 43

   Capitalization 45
   Abbreviations 50
   Word Division 53
   Numbers 55
   Punctuation 60
   State Abbreviations 69
   Proofreader's Marks 70
   Terminology 71

INTRODUCTION

A personal computer and word processing software are valuable tools for efficiently preparing letters and reports.

In addition to knowing about the computer and being skilled in the use of your word processing software program, it is equally important to adhere to correct business style in formatting your documents.

You will find this guide to be a handy reference tool that will enable you to prepare letters and reports that conform to the most up-to-date, acceptable formats.

P A R T

I

Letters

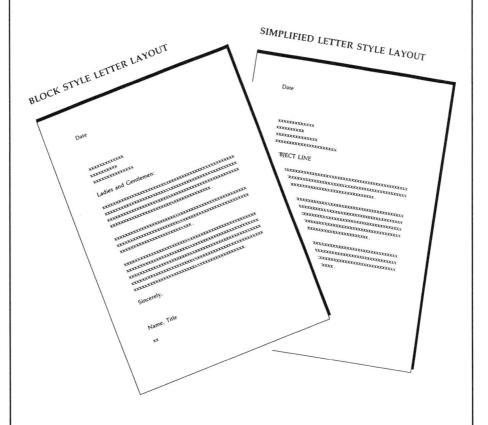

BLOCK STYLE LETTER LAYOUT

SIMPLIFIED LETTER STYLE LAYOUT

APPEARANCE OF THE LETTER

Your letters project both your personal image and the image of your company. It is important to adhere to the principles of effective business writing and to prepare letters that appear attractive on the page.

A business letter is usually printed on letterhead stationery. The letterhead typically includes the name, address and telephone number of the company or individual. It may also include a company logo or design.

The appearance of a letter is determined by:

▶ How the letter is placed on the page

▶ Letter style selected

▶ Correct usage of the required parts of a letter

▶ Correct usage of optional parts of a letter

This book contains information to help you prepare correct and professional-looking letters on a personal computer.

YOUR WORD PROCESSING SOFTWARE: WHAT YOU NEED TO KNOW

There are numerous word processing software programs on the market that enable you to perform basically the same functions. This guide is designed for use with *any* word processing program. It does *not* include specific commands or instructions related to specific programs.

You will, therefore, find it useful to take a few minutes to fill in the commands for your program. The procedures listed below are basic functions that you will use in preparing business letters:

Procedure	Fill in Commands for Your Program
Start up system	
Set line spacing	
Set left/right margins	
Tab set	
Caps lock	
Insert text	
Delete text	
Spell check	
Save document	
Print document	
Retrieve document	
Center horizontally	
Bold	
Underline	
Default settings	

LETTER PLACEMENT GUIDE

To create a favorable first impression on the reader, you will want to type your business letter attractively on the page:

- Set one inch left and right margins. For most software programs, you will use the default settings for left and right margins, which are generally 1 to 1½ inches.

- Type the date 2 inches from the top of the page or approximately ½ inch below the bottom of the letterhead design.

VERTICAL PLACEMENT

Because letters vary in length, you will want to make some choices about the vertical placement of your letter. The following guidelines will help you determine the vertical placement of your letters.

Spacing Between Date and Inside Address

Use the table below as a guide for the number of spaces to leave blank between the date and the inside address:

Letter Length	Number of Spaces between Date and Inside Address
Short: Under 100 words	8–10 line spaces
Average: 100–200 words	6–9 line spaces
Long: over 200 words	4–6 line spaces

Since the length of the letters within each of the three categories—short, average and long—varies considerably, you will have to use some judgment.

In general, for short letters, you can allow more space between the date and inside address, or increase the space between the letterhead and the dateline.

For longer letters, leave fewer spaces between the date and the inside address, or decrease the space between the letterhead and the dateline.

If your letter is extremely short (under 50 words), consider changing the left and right margins to 1½ inches.

LETTER PLACEMENT GUIDE (continued)

TWO-PAGE LETTERS

When a letter is longer than one page, leave only four to six spaces between the date and inside address. Use one-inch left and right margins on all pages.

Prepare the second page as follows:

- Use plain bond paper, the same color and quality as the letterhead.

- Use the same side margins (1 inch) as on page 1.

- Leave approximately a 1 inch margin at the bottom of page 1.

- Do not divide a paragraph between pages unless you can leave at least 2 lines of type both at the bottom of the first page and at the top of the second page.

- Do not hypenate the last word on page 1.

- Keep at least two lines of the last paragraph of the letter on the second page with the complimentary close.

- Begin typing the second page one inch from the top of the paper.

- Begin the second page with a heading, which contains identifying information in either of the following formats. Begin keyboarding at the left margin, 1 inch from the top of the page:

    Ms. Rachel S. Garrett (addressee)
    Page 2
    November 22, 199–

        or

    Ms. Rachel S. Garrett   2   November 22, 199–

- Quadruple space after the heading and continue keyboarding the letter.

HINTS FOR ADJUSTING THE LETTER PLACEMENT

You may need to make adjustments so your letter will appear balanced on the page:

To Shorten a Long Letter:

► Reduce the number of spaces between the letterhead and the date. Leave at least one blank line.

► Reduce the number of spaces between the date and the inside address. Leave at least two blank lines.

► Single space between the reference initials, enclosure notation and copy notation.

► Reduce the number of spaces allowed for the written signature.

To Lengthen a Short Letter:

► Increase the left and right margins to one and one-half or two inches.

► Increase the number of spaces between the letterhead and the date.

► Increase the number of spaces between the date and the inside address.

► Double- or triple-space between the reference initials, enclosure notation and copy notation.

► Increase the number of spaces left for the written signature.

REQUIRED PARTS OF A LETTER

DATE

The date tells the reader when the letter was written. Keyboard the date as the month, numerical day of the month, followed by a comma and the year. For example, January 1, 1992. Keyboard the date two inches from the top edge of the paper, either at the center of the page or at the left margin, depending on the style of the letter.

INSIDE ADDRESS

The inside address includes the addressee's name, title, company name, street number and name, city, state and ZIP code.

The first lines of the inside address contain the name of the person or the company addressed—the addressee. If the addressee's name, title and company name are all long, type the title on a separate line, after the name.

Mr. Gregory R. Johannson
Administrative Office Manager
Southeastern Manufacturing Company

Ms. Linda Jones, President
Southeastern Manufacturing Company

Mr. Gregory R. Johannson
President, Southern Press

Do not use abbreviations in the street address. Write out words such as North, South, East, West, Street and Avenue. However, it is appropriate to abbreviate NE, SW, etc., when these directional words follow the street address.

The last line of the inside address consists of the city, the two-letter state abbreviation, and the ZIP code. Always use the two-letter state abbreviation for the name of the state (see State Abbreviations). Leave two spaces between the state abbreviation and the ZIP code.

SALUTATION

The salutation is determined by the information given in the inside address. A salutation is not used in the simplified letter style.

When a letter is addressed to an individual, use the name of the individual with his or her title as the salutation.

Dear Mr. (Ms., Mrs., Dr. or Professor) _____

When a letter is addressed to a company, use the salutation "Ladies and Gentlemen."

Do Not Use: Gentlemen:
Dear Sir:
Dear Madame:
Dear Sir or Madame:
To Whom it May Concern:

BODY OF THE LETTER

The body of the letter contains the message. Begin keyboarding paragraphs at the left margin; modified block style letters may begin with the first line of the paragraph indented one-half inch. Each paragraph is single spaced with a double space—one blank line—between paragraphs. For example:

Date

ABC Publishing Company
3425 West 57 Street
New York, NY 10023

Ladies and Gentlemen:

xxxxxxxxxxxxxxxxxxxxxxxxxxxxxxxxxxxxxxxxxxxxxxxxxxxxxxxxxxxxxxxx
xxxxxxxxxxxxxxxxxxxxxxxxxxxxxxxxxxxxxxxxxxxxxxxxxxxxxxxxxxxxxxxx
xxxxxxxxxxxxxxxxxxxxxxxxxxxxxxxxxxxxxxxxxxxxxxxxxxx.

REQUIRED PARTS OF A LETTER (continued)

COMPLIMENTARY CLOSE

Choose a complimentary close consistent with the nature and tone of your letter. For example, *Sincerely* is more friendly and casual than *Very truly yours.* Frequently used closings include: Sincerely, Cordially and Very truly yours.

Do not use a complimentary close in the simplified letter style (see Letter Styles).

SIGNATURE LINE

The signature line identifies the writer of the letter and may include the writer's title and department. Three blank lines are left after the complimentary close to allow space for the written signature.

The signature line may consist of one or two lines. If the name and the title are relatively short, they may appear together on one line, separated by a comma. If they are long, two lines are more attractive. If possible, you want to achieve a well-balanced effect.

Lynn King   Lawrence A. Gregory
Judy Davis, President   Vice President of Marketing

REFERENCE INITIALS

Use reference initials to identify the typist who prepares the communication. Type them in lowercase letters, double-spaced below the signature line:

xxxxxxxxxxxxxxxxxxxxxxxxxxxxxxxxxxxxxxxxxxxxxxxxxxxxxxxxxxxxxxxx
xxxxxxxxxxxxxxxxxxxxxxxxxxxxxxxxxxxxxxxxxxxxxxxxxxxxxxxxxxxxxxxx
xxxxxxxxxxxxxxxxxxxxxxxxxxxxxxxxxxxxxxxxxxxxxxxxxxxxxx.

Sincerely yours,

Larry D. Randolph, President

rdh

LETTER STYLES

A variety of letter styles are acceptable for business and personal letters. This section introduces four basic styles that are very similar; the style you choose will be determined either by your personal preference or a preference expressed by your employer.

The **Block Style Letter** is very popular. It is easy to format, as all lines begin at the left margin.

The **Modified Block Style Letter** is the most traditional of the letter styles shown. It is similar to the block style, differing only in the placement of the date, complimentary close and signature. Although the modified block style letter can be keyboarded with indented paragraphs, it is most often prepared today with block paragraphs.

The **Simplified Letter Style** is becoming more widely acceptable because of its ease of preparation. It meets resistance from more traditional business writers who consider the omission of the salutation and complimentary close too impersonal. On the other hand, it is becoming an acceptable way of handling the problem of determining the appropriate salutation (see Salutation).

In the **Social Business Letter** the message is more social than business and/or the writer and the recipient of the letter have a social as well as business relationship. Plain paper is used, in place of the company letterhead, and the return address is typed directly above the date. Both the block and modified block style formats are appropriate for this type of letter.

Punctuation Styles

The two forms of punctuation for business letters are *mixed* and *open* punctuation.

Mixed Punctuation — Use a colon after the salutation and a comma after the complimentary close. This is the most widely acceptable punctuation style. Examples include:

> Ladies and Gentlemen:
> Dear Ms. Morris:
> Sincerely yours,

Open Punctuation — Do not keyboard punctuation after the salutation and the complimentary close. For example:

> Ladies and Gentlemen
> Dear Ms. Morris
> Sincerely yours

BLOCK STYLE LETTER

Step-by-Step Instructions

Adjust software settings:

- Set line spacing for single spacing
- Set one inch left and right margins

To Keyboard a Letter:

1. Use the ENTER key to space down one inch from the top margin setting.

2. Keyboard the date at the left margin.

3. Press ENTER as appropriate to leave space between the date and the inside address (see Letter Placement Guide).

4. Keyboard inside address at the left margin.

5. Press ENTER twice.

6. Keyboard the salutation.

7. Press ENTER twice.

8. Keyboard the body of the letter, beginning each paragraph at the left margin. Press ENTER twice at the end of each paragraph.

9. Keyboard the complimentary close.

10. Press ENTER four times.

11. Keyboard the writer's name (and title, if appropriate).

12. Press ENTER twice.

13. Keyboard your initials.

BLOCK STYLE LETTER LAYOUT

Date

 xxxxxxxxxxxx
xxxxxxxxx
xxxxxxxxxxxxxx

Ladies and Gentlemen:

xxxxxxxxxxxxxxxxxxxxxxxxxxxxxxxxxxxxxxxxxxxxxxx
xxxxxxxxxxxxxxxxxxxxxxxxxxxxxxxxxxxxxxxxxxxxxxx
xxxxxxxxxxxxxxxxxxxxxxxxxxxxxxxxxxxxxxxxxxxxx
 xxxxxxxxxxxxxxxxxxxxxxxxxxxxxxxxxxxxx .

xxxxxxxxxxxxxxxxxxxxxxxxxxxxxxxxxxxxxxxxxxxxxxx
xxxxxxxxxxxxxxxxxxxxxxxxxxxxxxxxxxxxxxxxxxxxxxx
 xxxxxxxxxxxxxxxxxxxxxxxxxxx .

xxxxxxxxxxxxxxxxxxxxxxxxxxxxxxxxxxxxxxxxxxxxxxx
xxxxxxxxxxxxxxxxxxxxxxxxxxxxxxxxxxxxxxxxxxxxxxx
xxxxxxxxxxxxxxxxxxxxxxxxxxxxxxxxxxxxxxxxxxxxx
xxxxxxxxxxxxxxxxxxxxxxxxxxxxxxxxxxxxxxxxxxxxxxx
xxxxxxxxxxxxxxxxxxxxxxxxxxxxxxxxxxxxxxxxxxxx.

Sincerely,

Name, Title

xx

MODIFIED BLOCK STYLE LETTER

Step-by-Step Instructions

Adjust software settings:

- Set line spacing for single spacing
- Set one inch left and right margins
- Set tab at center point as identified by your software program

To Keyboard a Letter:

1. Use the ENTER key to space down one inch from the top margin setting.

2. Press TAB to move the cursor to the center point. Keyboard the date.

3. Press ENTER as appropriate to leave space between the date and the inside address (see Letter Placement Guide).

4. Keyboard the inside address at the left margin.

5. Press ENTER twice.

6. Keyboard the salutation.

7. Press ENTER twice.

8. Keyboard the body of the letter, beginning each paragraph at the left margin. Press ENTER twice at the end of each paragraph.

9. Press TAB to move the cursor to the center point. Keyboard the complimentary close.

10. Press ENTER four times, leaving three blank lines for the writer's signature.

11. Press the TAB key to move the cursor to the center point. Keyboard the writer's name (and title, if appropriate).

12. Press ENTER twice.

13. Keyboard your initials at the left margin.

MODIFIED BLOCK STYLE LETTER LAYOUT

Date

xxxxxxxxxxxx
xxxxxxxxx
xxxxxxxxxxxxx
xxxxxxxxxxxxxxxxxxxxx

Ladies and Gentlemen:

xxxxxxxxxxxxxxxxxxxxxxxxxxxxxxxxxxxxxxxxxxxxxx
xxxxxxxxxxxxxxxxxxxxxxxxxxxxxxxxxxxxxxxxxxxxx.

xxxxxxxxxxxxxxxxxxxxxxxxxxxxxxxxxxxxxxxxxxxxxx
xxxxxxxxxxxxxxxxxxxxxxxxxxxxxxxxxxxxxxxxxxxxxx
xxxxxxxxxxxxxxxxxxxxxxxxxxxxxxxxxxxxxxxxxxxxxx
xxxxxxxxxxxxxxxxxxxxxxxxxxxxxxxxxx.

xxxxxxxxxxxxxxxxxxxxxxxxxxxxxxxxxxxxxxxxxxxxxx
xxxxxxxxxxxxxxxxxxxxxxxxxxxxxxxxxxxxxxxxxxxxxx
xxxxxxxxxxxxxxxxxxxxxxxxxxxxxxxxxxxxxxxxxxxxxx
xxxxxxxxxxxxxxxxxxxxxxxxxxxxxxxxxxxxxxxxxxxxxx
xxxxxxxxxxxxxxxxxxxxxxxxxxxxxx.

Sincerely,

Name, Title

xx

SIMPLIFIED LETTER

Step-by-Step Instructions

Adjust software settings:

- Set line spacing for single spacing
- Set one inch left and right margins

To Keyboard a Letter:

1. Use the ENTER key to space down one inch from the top margin setting.

2. Keyboard the date at the left margin.

3. Press ENTER as appropriate to leave space between the date and the inside address (see Letter Placement Guide).

4. Keyboard the inside address at the left margin.

5. Press ENTER twice.

6. Keyboard the subject line, all uppercase.

7. Press ENTER twice.

8. Keyboard the body of the letter, beginning each paragraph at the left margin. Press ENTER twice between paragraphs.

9. After keyboarding the last paragraph, press ENTER four times.

10. Keyboard the writer's name, a comma and title, all uppercase.

11. Press ENTER twice.

12. Keyboard your initials.

SIMPLIFIED LETTER STYLE LAYOUT

Date

 xxxxxxxxxxxx
xxxxxxxxx
xxxxxxxxxxxxxx
 xxxxxxxxxxxxxxxxxxxxxxx

SUBJECT LINE

xxxxxxxxxxxxxxxxxxxxxxxxxxxxxxxxxxxxxxxxxxxxxxxxxx
xxxxxxxxxxxxxxxxxxxxxxxxxxxxxxxxxxxxxxxxxxxxxxxxxx
xxxxxxxxxxxxxxxxxxxxxxxxxxxxxxxxxxxx .

xxxxxxxxxxxxxxxxxxxxxxxxxxxxxxxxxxxxxxxxxxxxxxxxxx
xxxxxxxxxxxxxxxxxxxxxxxxxxxxxxxxxxxxxxxxxxxxxxxxxx
xxxxxxxxxxxxxxxxxxxxxxxxxxxxxxxxxxxxxxxxxxxxxxxxxx
xxxxxxxxxxxxxxxxxxxxxxxxxxxxxxxxxxxxxxxxxxxxxxxxxx
xxxxxxxxxxxxxxxxxxxxxxxxxxxxxxxxxxxxx .

xxxxxxxxxxxxxxxxxxxxxxxxxxxxxxxxxxxxxxxxxxxxxxxxxx
xxxxxxxxxxxxxxxxxxxxxxxxxxxxxxxxxxxxxxxxxxxxxxxxxx
xxxxxxxxxxxxxxxxxxxxxxxxxxxxxxxxxxxxxxxxxxxxxxxxxx
 xxxxxxxxxxxxxxxxxxxxxxxxxxxxx .

NAME, TITLE

xx

OPTIONAL PARTS OF A LETTER

The following parts of a business letter are optional and are only included in a letter when needed or desired. When appropriate, keyboard them according to the formatting guidelines below:

MAILING AND OTHER SPECIAL NOTATIONS

When you want to indicate on the letter the mail service used—envelopes are usually discarded when the mail is opened—keyboard mailing (Registered, Special Delivery, Certified) and other special notations (Personal, Confidential), all uppercase, at the left margin, double-spaced below the dateline.

ATTENTION LINE

When a letter is addressed to a company, an attention line often directs the letter to a particular person or department. The attention line indicates that the writer prefers that the letter be handled by the person or department named in the attention line, whenever possible.

- Keyboard the attention line as the second line of the inside address, immediately following the company name.

- Acceptable styles for the attention line:
  —Attention Ms. Barbara Curtis
  —ATTENTION Ms. Barbara Curtis
  —Attention: Larry Mann
  —ATTENTION: Larry Mann

SUBJECT LINE

A subject line serves as a title to the letter. It may be used to draw the reader's attention to an item of importance.

- Keyboard the subject line a double space below the salutation. Double space before keyboarding the body of the letter. The subject line is usually placed at the left margin, but can be centered when using the modified block style letter.

- Keyboard the subject line, all uppercase, or in upper- and lowercase. The word *SUBJECT* or *RE,* followed by a colon, may be used with the subject line, but is not required.

Acceptable styles for the subject line:

—Information Processing Conference

—INFORMATION PROCESSING CONFERENCE

—SUBJECT: Information Processing Conference

—RE: INFORMATION PROCESSING CONFERENCE

COMPANY NAME

Some organizations include the company name as part of the closing:

- Keyboard the company name in uppercase, double-spaced after the Complimentary close and at the same position horizontally (at the left margin or centered).

ENCLOSURE NOTATION

The word *Enclosure* tells the reader that something is being enclosed in the envelope with the letter. If more than one item is enclosed, use the plural *Enclosures* or list each item.

- Keyboard the enclosure notation at the left margin, double-spaced below the reference initials.

- Acceptable styles for enclosure notations:
  —Enclosure
  —Enc.
  —Enclosures (2)
  —Encs.
  —Enclosures: Purchase Order
                    Invoice

OPTIONAL PARTS OF A LETTER (continued)

COPY NOTATION

When copies of a letter are sent to individuals other than the addressee, use a copy notation.

- Keyboard the copy notation at the left margin, double-spaced below the enclosure notation or reference initials, whichever is last.

- Use either the notation *c* or *pc* (photocopy).

- If more than one person is to receive a copy, list the names after the copy notation.

Acceptable styles for the copy notation:

—c David C. Ryan

—pc Rachel S. Collins

—c Elizabeth Roberts, Director of Marketing
    John Casey, Director of Advertising
    Nancy Bowden, Sales Manager

BLIND COPY NOTATION

When you want to send a copy of a letter to a person without informing the addressee, use a blind copy notation.

- Keyboard the notation on the file copy only.

- Keyboard the notation as *bc,* or *bpc.*

- Keyboard this notation in the same place as the copy notation.

POSTSCRIPT

A postscript is an additional message sometimes added at the end of a letter.

- Keyboard the postscript as the last item on the letter, double-spaced below the last item on the page.

- Keyboard the postscript using the same paragraph style as the body of the letter—block or indented.

LETTER FORMAT WITH OPTIONAL PARTS

Date

CERTIFIED MAIL

ABC Company
Attention Kenneth Bauer
xxxxxxxxxx
xxxxxxxxxxxxxxx

Ladies and Gentlemen:

INFORMATION PROCESSING CONFERENCE

xxxxxxxxxxxxxxxxxxxxxxxxxxxxxxxxxxxxxxxxxxxxxxxxx
xxxxxxxxxxxxxxxxxxxxxxxxxxxxxxxxxxxxxxxxxxxxxxx.

xxxxxxxxxxxxxxxxxxxxxxxxxxxxxxxxxxxxxxxxxxxxxxxxx
xxxxxxxxxxxxxxxxxxxxxxxxxxxxxxxxxxxxxxxxxxxxxxxxx
xxxxxxxxxxxxxxxxxxxxxxxxxxxxxxxxxxxxxxxxxxxxxxxxx
xxxxxxxxxxxxxxxxxxxxxxxxxxxxxxxxxxxxxxxx.

Sincerely,

XYZ Company

Name, Title

rdh

Enc.

c Michael Collins, Reservations Manager

Postscript keyboarded here, matching the paragraph style.

ENVELOPES

To use your computer to address envelopes, follow the specific directions given for your word processing software and for your printer.

RETURN ADDRESS

Business envelopes usually contain the name and address of the company in the upper left-hand corner of the envelope. In large offices, the name and/or department of the writer may be keyboarded above the printed return address.

If your office does not have preprinted envelopes or if you are writing personal business letters, keyboard the return address in the upper left-hand corner of the envelope. Keyboard the return address a double space below the top edge of the envelope and one-half inch from the left edge.

MAILING ADDRESS

The mailing address on the envelope should be keyboarded exactly as it appears on the letter.

► **Placement**

On a Large (No. 10) envelope, keyboard the mailing address, 4 inches from the left edge and 2½ inches from the top edge.

On a Small (No. 6¾) envelope, keyboard the address 2½ inches from the left edge and 2 inches from the top edge.

► **Format**

The U.S. Postal Service prefers that envelope addresses be keyboarded in all capital letters, without punctuation. Single space the address.

The city, state, and ZIP code should be the last line of the address. Use the two-letter state abbreviation (see State Abbreviations), and leave one or two spaces between the state abbreviation and the ZIP code.

The Post Office recommends using the expanded nine-digit ZIP code, which speeds mail processing.

ATTENTION LINE

An attention line may be used when a letter is addressed to a company, but the writer wants to direct it to an individual in the company. The attention line should be keyboarded as a part of the mailing address, immediately below the name of the company.

WORLD PUBLISHING COMPANY
ATTENTION MS. SHARON R. GREGORY

ADDRESSEE NOTATIONS

Addressee notations include information such as CONFIDENTIAL, PERSONAL, HOLD FOR ARRIVAL, PLEASE FORWARD. These notations are intended for the use of the person or office receiving the mail. These notations should be keyboarded in all capital letters, ½ inch from the left edge of envelope and ½ inch below the return address.

MAILING NOTATIONS

Mailing notations are directions for the Postal Service, such as CERTIFIED, REGISTERED, SPECIAL DELIVERY. These notations should be keyboarded in all capital letters, below the postage stamp, approximately 1½ inches from the top edge of the envelope.

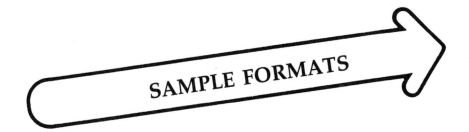

SAMPLE FORMATS

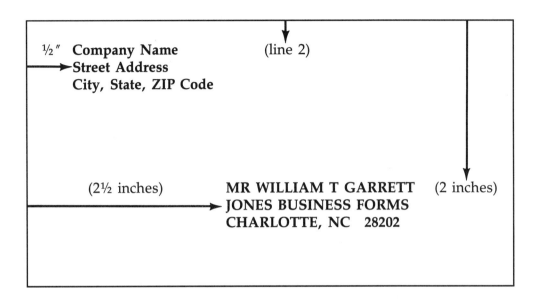

SAMPLE ENVELOPE LAYOUTS

½″ **Company Name**
   Street Address
   City, State, ZIP Code

(line 2)

(2½ inches)   **MR WILLIAM T GARRETT**   (2 inches)
            JONES BUSINESS FORMS
            CHARLOTTE, NC   28202

No. 6¾ Envelope

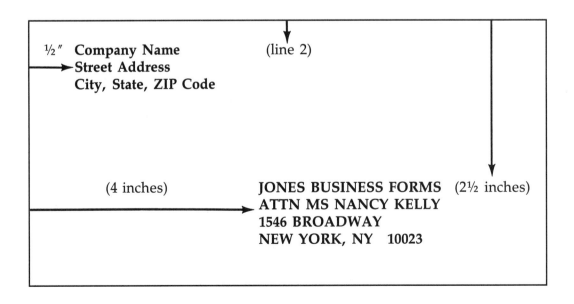

½″ **Company Name**
   Street Address
   City, State, ZIP Code

(line 2)

(4 inches)   **JONES BUSINESS FORMS** (2½ inches)
           ATTN MS NANCY KELLY
           1546 BROADWAY
           NEW YORK, NY   10023

No. 10 Envelope

26

P A R T

II

Reports

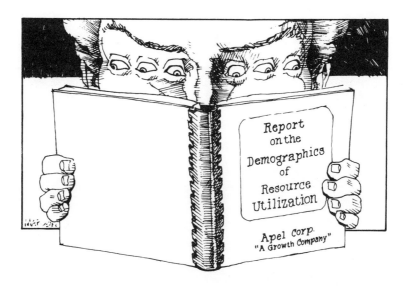

REPORT FORMAT AND WORD PROCESSING SOFTWARE

The guidelines presented in this section represent the standard report format. However, because of the variety of word processing software available today and the various default settings used, you may want to deviate from the guidelines suggested.

Learn the features of your software and use them to make your report preparation easier and to enhance the appearance of your reports.

YOUR WORD PROCESSING SOFTWARE: WHAT YOU NEED TO KNOW

Formatting a report involves some additional features of your word processing program. Before preparing a report, review the word processing features you listed on page 6, and familiarize yourself with the procedures listed below.

Fill in the commands listed below, for your program. These features will be useful in preparing reports.

Procedures	Fill in Commands for Your Program
Top/bottom margins	
Center horizontally	
Underscore	
Bold print	
Page breaks	
Page numbers	
Headers/footers	
Indent left and right	
Superscripts	
Footnotes	
Endnotes	
Fonts	
Borders	
Graphics	

FORMAT FOR REPORTS

SPACING

Double-spaced reports are easiest to read. Tab to indent the first line of each paragraph ½ inch from the left margin.

MARGINS

Unbound Report:

• Set 1 inch left and right margins.

• Set 1 inch top margin for all pages except page 1, which should begin 1½ inches from the page top.

• Set 1 inch bottom margin on all pages.

Top Bound Report:

• Set 1 inch left and right margins.

• Set 2 inch top margin on page 1. Set 1½ inch margin on all other pages to allow an extra ½ inch for the binding.

• Set 1 inch bottom margin on all pages.

Left Bound Report:

• Set 1½ inch margin on all pages to allow for the binding. Set 1 inch right margin.

• Set 1½ inch top margin on page 1. Set 1 inch top margins on all other pages.

• Set 1 inch bottom margin on all pages.

FORMAT FOR REPORTS (continued)

HEADINGS

Title:
- Keyboard the title of the report, in capital letters, centered horizontally on the page.
- Quadruple space after the title if there is no secondary heading.

Secondary Heading:
- Center the heading horizontally.
- Capitalize the first letter of each major word.
- Double-space before the heading and quadruple space after the heading.

Side Heading:
- Keyboard the heading at the left margin.
- Underscore the heading and capitalize the first letter of each major word.
- Double-space before and after the heading.

Paragraph Heading:
- Double-space before the heading.
- Indent from the left margin and capitalize the first letter of the first word.
- Underscore the heading and end with a period.

REPORT TITLE

Secondary Heading

Side Heading

xxxxxxxxxxxxxxxxxxxxxxxxxxxxxxxxxxxxxxxxxxxxxxxxxxxxxxxxxxxxxx

xxxxxxxxxxxxxxxxxxxxxxxxxxxxxxxxxxxxxxxxxxxxxxxxxxxxxxxxxxxxxx.

Paragraph heading. xxxxxxxxxxxxxxxxxxxxxxxxxxxxxxxxxxxxxxxxxxx

xxxxxxxxxxxxxxxxxxxxxxxxxxxxxxxxxxxxxxxxxxxxxxxxxxxxxxx.

PAGINATION

The page number is usually omitted from the first page. Beginning with page 2 of the report, keyboard the page number either ½ inch from the bottom of the page at the center, or ½ inch from the top edge at the right margin.

ENUMERATIONS

Enumerations—or listings—are indented ½ inch from the left and right margins. Double space before and after each of the items. Single space items longer than 1 line; begin the second and succeeding lines under the first word, *not* the number.

xxxxxxxxxxxxxxxxxxxxxxxxxxxxxxxxxxxxxxxxxxxxxxxxxxxxxxxxxxxxxxxxx

xxxxxxxxxxxxxxxxxxxxxxxxxxxxxxxxxxxxxxxxxxxxxxxxxxxxxxxx.

1. xxxxxxxxxxxxxxxxxxxxxxxxxxxxxxxxxxxxxxxxxxxxxxxxxxxxx
xxxxxxxxxxxxxxxxxxxxxxxxxxxxxxxxxxxxxxxxxxxxxxxxxxxx .

2. xxxxxxxxxxxxxxxxxxxxxxxxxxxxxxxxxxxxxxxxxxxxxxxxxxxxx
xxxxxxxxxxxxxxxxxxxxxxxxxxxxxxxxxxxx .

QUOTATIONS

When a quotation is longer than 2 lines, it is indented ½ inch from the left and right margins and is single spaced. Quoted material is preceded and followed by a double space.

xxxxxxxxxxxxxxxxxxxxxxxxxxxxxxxxxxxxxxxxxxxxxxxxxxxxxxxxxxxxx

xxxxxxxxxxxxxxxxxxxxxxxxxxxxxxxxxxxxxxxxxxxxxxxxxxxxxxxxxxxxx.

xxxxxxxxxxxxxxxxxxxxxxxxxxxxxxxxxxxxxxxxxxxxxxxxxxxxxxxxxx
xxxxxxxxxxxxxxxxxxxxxxxxxxxxxxxxxxxxxxxxxxxxxxxxxxxxxxxxxx
xxxxxxxxxxxxxxxxxxxxxxxxxxxxxxxxxxxxxxxxxxxxxxx .

DOCUMENTING SOURCES USED IN PREPARING YOUR REPORT

A number of styles are accepted for citing sources used in your report. Your choice of style depends on the academic discipline, a style preference of your company, or the capabilities of your software program. Regardless of the method you select, consult a reference manual for further information and be consistent throughout your document.

The guidelines that follow describe briefly how to document sources using footnotes, endnotes and internal citations. In general, footnotes and endnotes include the following information:

- name of author

- title

- name of publisher

- place and date of publication

- page number(s) containing the information

Although formats for keyboarding this information vary according to different reference manuals, the following are examples of accepted formats:

Book (one author)

Kenneth E. Blanchard, The One Minute Manager (New York: Morrow, 1987), p. 36.

Book (two authors)

Thomas J. Peters and Robert H. Waterman, Jr., In Search of Excellence (New York: Harper & Row, 1982), p. 87.

Magazine Article

Morgan W. McCall, Jr., and Michael M. Lombardo, ''What Makes a Top Executive?'' Psychology Today (February 1983), p. 26.

Interview

```
    Interview with Dr. James Bronner, Professor, New York, New York,
June 14, 1991.
```

Personal Correspondence

```
    Professor Janet Swarth, January 22, 1991, personal correspondence.
```

FOOTNOTES

Footnotes are traditionally numbered within the text with a superior or superscript number and keyboarded at the bottom of the report page. Unless your software has a footnote feature that automatically places a footnote at the bottom of the page on which the reference is cited, it is recommended that you prepare footnotes as endnotes (see below).

ENDNOTES

Endnotes are similar to footnotes. Instead of being placed at the bottom of each page, they are placed on a separate page at the end of the report. The page is headed with the word ENDNOTES, followed by a quadruple space.

INTERNAL CITATIONS

Another option is to use internal citations, where quoted material is cited within the report. Only the author's surname and the year of publication are identified. The page number of the reference is included in a bibliography (or Reference List) that follows the report.

    . . . . xxxxxxxxxxxxxxx.'' (Berne, 1984).

DOCUMENTING SOURCES USED IN PREPARING YOUR REPORT (continued)

BIBLIOGRAPHY

A separate bibliography page identifies all sources used in the report. Title the page *Bibliography* and quadruple space following the title.

- Single space each item

- Double-space between items

- Begin the first line of each item at the left margin

- Indent the second and subsequent lines one-half inch from the left margin

- List entries alphabetically according to the last name of the author

The specific format for the entries may vary according to the type of source cited. Consult a reference manual for the specific format for bibliographic entries.

BIBLIOGRAPHY

Adler, Jerry, ''The House of the Future,'' <u>Newsweek</u>, Winter/Spring 1990, p. 72.

Berne, Eric, <u>What Do You Say After You Say Hello?</u> New York: Ballantine, 1984.

SAMPLE LAYOUTS

Page with Footnotes

xxxxxxxxxxxxxxxxxxxxxxxxxxxxxxxxxxxxxxxxxxxxxxxxxxxxxxxxxxxxx
xxxxxxxxxxxxxxxxxxxxxxxxxxxxxxxxxxxxxxxxxxxxxxxxxxxxxxxxxxxxx
xxxxxxxxxxxxxxxxxxxxxxxxxxxxxxxxxxxxxxxxxxxxxxxxxxx.[1]
xxxxxxxxxxxxxxxxxxxxxxxxxxxxxxxxxxxxxxxxxxxxxxxxxxxxxxxx
xxxxxxxxxxxxxxxxxxxxxxxxxxxxxxxxxxxxxxx .[2]

---

[1]Eric Berne, <u>What Do You Say After You Say Hello?</u> (New York: Ballantine, 1984), p. 55.

[2]Jerry Adler, ''The House of the Future,'' <u>Newsweek</u> (Winter/Spring 1990), p. 72.

Page with Endnotes

xxxxxxxxxxxxxxxxxxxxxxxxxxxxxxxxxxxxxxxxxxxxxxxxxxxxxxxxxxxxxxxx
xxxxxxxxxxxxxxxxxxxxxxxxxxxxxxxxxxxxxxxxxxxxxxxxxxxxxxxxxxxxxxxx
xxxxxxxxxxxxxxxxxxxxxxxxxxxxxxxxxxxxxxxxxxxxxxxxxxxxxxxxx.[1]
xxxxxxxxxxxxxxxxxxxxxxxxxxxxxxxxxxxxxxxxxxxxxxxxxxxxxxxx
xxxxxxxxxxxxxxxxxxxxxxxxxxxxxxxxxxxxxxx .[2]

ENDNOTES

1. Eric Berne, <u>What Do You Say After You Say Hello?</u> (New York: Ballantine, 1984), p. 55.

2. Jerry Adler, ''The House of the Future,'' <u>Newsweek</u> (Winter/Spring 1990), p. 72.

ADDITIONAL PARTS OF A REPORT

A report may include the following parts, in addition to the body:

- Title Page
- Table of Contents
- List of Illustrations and Tables
- Bibliography
- Appendix

TITLE PAGE

The title page generally contains the title of the report, the writer's name, title and department, and the date the report is submitted. Other information may be included if desired.

- Center horizontally each of the lines of the title page

- Keyboard the title in capital letters, about two inches from the top of the page.

- If the title is more than one line, single space the additional lines

The other items are keyboarded to achieve balance, leaving a two-inch margin at the bottom of the page. Depending on the nature and formality of the report, graphics and borders may be used to create an attractive title page.

TABLE OF CONTENTS

The table of contents lists the major divisions of a report and the page number of the first page of each of the divisions. The heading is keyboarded in capital letters and centered 1½ inches from the top of the page.

- Use the same left and right margins as you use for the report.

- Double-space after the title and each major division and single space between subdivisions.

- Use leaders (. . . .) to make it easier to read across to the page number. Leaders are a series of periods, each followed by a space. The periods must line up under each other.

- Number the table of contents page with a lowercase Roman numeral at the bottom of the page.

LIST OF ILLUSTRATIONS AND TABLES

When a report contains several illustrations or tables, it is useful to prepare a list so they can be located easily. Prepare the list on a separate page, following the table of contents. Begin with the heading, keyboarded in capital letters centered 1½ inches from the top of the page.

- Keyboard the word *Illustration* or *Table* at the left margin.

- Keyboard the word *Page* at the right margin.

- Keyboard the title of each Illustration in capital letters.

- Single space each title.

- Double-space between titles.

- Leaders may be used between titles and page numbers.

- Number the list at the bottom of the page with a lowercase Roman numeral.

APPENDIX

The appendix consists of documents that support the report, such as letters, tables, lists, questionnaires or other materials. It follows the bibliography and often includes a page with the title *Appendix,* keyboarded in capital letters. This page may list items contained in the appendix, numbered with alphabetic letters.

SAMPLE LAYOUTS

SAMPLE TITLE PAGE

DOCUMENT PREPARATION ON THE COMPUTER

Cody H. Garrett
Director, Communications Systems

April 26, 1992

SAMPLE TABLE OF CONTENTS PAGE

TABLE OF CONTENTS

Acknowledgments ii

List of Tables iii

  I. INTRODUCTION 1

 II. LETTER STYLES 4

      A. The Block Style Letter 6
      B. The Modified Block Style Letter 8
      C. The Simplified Letter Style 10

III. REQUIRED PARTS OF A LETTER 12

      A. Date 12
      B. Inside Address 13
      C. Salutation 13
      D. Body of the Letter 14
      E. Complimentary Close 14
      F. Signature Line 15
      G. Reference Initials 15

i

SAMPLE LIST OF ILLUSTRATIONS PAGE

LIST OF ILLUSTRATIONS

Illustration   Page

1. BLOCK STYLE LETTER 7

2. MODIFIED BLOCK STYLE LETTER 9

3. SIMPLIFIED LETTER 11

4. LETTER WITH OPTIONAL PARTS 15

5. ENVELOPES 21

iii

P A R T

III

Writing Tips

CAPITALIZATION

The current trend in writing is to avoid the heavy use of capitalization. Although authorities frequently disagree on the correct use of capital letters, these general rules reflect correct business usage:

NAMES

1. Capitalize *proper* nouns—the official name of a person, place or thing—and adjectives derived from proper nouns.

   United States   American
   France   French
   The University of Virginia

2. Capitalize names of organizations and institutions.

   International Business Machines
   Mt. Sinai Medical Center
   Association of Information Systems Professionals

   Note: Do not capitalize terms such as *company, corporation, committee* and *club* when they stand alone, unless special distinction is necessary, as in legal documents, bylaws or other uses in which the short form represents the full authority of the organization (such as the Club).

   an officer of the company
   a member of the committee

3. Capitalize the *full* name of places, not the short forms.

   Lake Michigan   the lake
   the Empire State Building   the building

   Note: A few short forms are capitalized because they are clearly associated with one place.

   the Coast   the West Coast
   the Canal   the Panama Canal

CAPITALIZATION (continued)

TITLES

4. Capitalize all official titles of honor and respect when they *precede* personal names.

President Carol Schein
Professor James Carleton

Note: Do *not* capitalize when the personal name is in apposition with the title or when the title follows the personal name.

our professor, James Carleton
the president of the company, Carol Schein

5. Always capitalize the title of high ranking national, state, and international officials, even when they follow or replace a name.

the Secretary of State
The Governor
The Prime Minister

Note: Always capitalize the following: President, Vice President, the Chief Justice, Cabinet members, Ambassadors, Senators, Representatives, Governor, Lieutenant Governor, Kings, Queens, and Secretary General of the United Nations.

PLACES

6. Capitalize *state* only when it follows the name of a state, *city* only when it is part of the corporate name of a city, and *the* only when it is part of the official name of a place.

New York State   the state of California
Garden City   the city of Charlotte
The Vatican

DEPARTMENTS

7. Capitalize organizational terms—names of departments or divisions—only when they are the office name.

    Department of Finance   your accounting department
    Department of Psychology

REGIONS

8. Capitalize *north, south, east, west,* etc., when they are used to designate definite regions. Do *not* capitalize them when they are used to indicate a general direction.

    the Midwest   turn east
    the South   drive north

DAYS, MONTHS

9. Capitalize the days of the week, the months of the year, and the names of holidays.

    Monday
    July
    Labor Day

ACADEMIC DEGREES

10. Capitalize academic degrees when used after a person's name but *not* when they are used as a general term of classification.

    Doctor of Philosophy   a master of science degree
    Janet W. Hubbard, Ph.D.   a bachelor of arts degree

CAPITALIZATION (continued)

NOUNS FOLLOWED BY NUMBERS

11. Capitalize a noun followed by a number or a letter that indicates sequence—except line, page, note, paragraph, size and verse.

> Chapter V
> Column 2
> Check 6804
> Invoice 32587
> Room 2008
> Policy 6790776
> Exhibit H

Note: It is usually unnecessary to use No. before the number, except with License, Patent and Social Security numbers.

> License No. 45-3355
> Social Security No. 167-58-3405

PUBLICATIONS

12. Capitalize the first and last word and all other words of the title of a publication except in short articles, conjunctions and prepositions that consist of fewer than four letters.

> *Modern Office Procedures*
> *Travel and Leisure*
> *A Manual of Style*

Note: Capitalize *the* at the beginning of a title only if it is actually part of the title.

> *The New York Times*

PRODUCT NAMES

13. Capitalize brand names, trademarks and commercial product names. Common names following the product names should not ordinarily be capitalized. However, advertisers and manufacturers often capitalize such words for special emphasis. Do *not* capitalize trade names that have become established as common nouns.

Panasonic typewriter   nylon
Philco television   kleenex

GOVERNMENT AGENCIES

14. Capitalize the words *federal* and *national* only when they are part of a proper name, such as the official name of a government agency. The terms *government* and *federal government*, referring to the United States government, are usually only capitalized in formal writing.

Federal Bureau of Investigation   the federal government
National Labor Relations Board   national elections

15. Capitalize the names of departments of the government, the official names of government bodies, and the titles of government documents.

Department of Justice
House of Representatives
Central Intelligence Agency

ABBREVIATIONS

As a general rule, abbreviate as little as possible.

1. Titles with surnames

When only the surname is used in a sentence, spell out all titles except Mr., Mrs., Ms., Dr. and Esq.

> Ms. Wilkes was invited to the lecture by Professor Morrow.

When using an initial or initials within an individual's name, capitalize the initial and follow it with a period and a space.

> Cody G. Crawford
> C. G. Crawford

Abbreviate Junior (Jr.) and Senior (Sr.) following personal names. Abbreviate or spell out Esquire (Esq.). Do not use a personal title such as Mr. or Ms. with Esq.

> Mr. John Gregory, Sr.
> John Gregory, Esquire
> Ellen Baer, Esq.

2. Academic degrees

Abbreviations of academic degrees require a period after each element in the abbreviation, but need no internal spaces.

> M.S.   M.D.   Ph.D.   D.D.S.

When an academic title follows an individual's name, do not use titles such as Ms., Mr. or Dr. before the name.

> Janet Rosen, Ph.D. (not Dr. Janet Rosen, Ph.D.)

3. Names of organizations

Write the name of an organization the way it is preferred by the group. To be accurate, use the letterhead of the organization as an example.

Names of well-known business organizations, labor unions, societies and associations are often abbreviated, except in the most formal writing. When these abbreviations contain all-capital letters, they are keyboarded without periods or spaces.

EEOC   Equal Employment Opportunity Commission
IBM   International Business Machines
NOW   National Organization for Women

4. Government agencies, radio and television stations

Do *not* use periods or spaces between letters indicating the names of government boards or after the call letters of radio or television stations.

NBC   National Broadcasting Company
CIA   Central Intelligence Agency
UN   United Nations

5. Compass points

Spell out compass points when they are used as ordinary nouns and adjectives.

They have returned from the convention in the Midwest.

Spell out compass points when they are included in street names.

The meeting will be held at their office at 459 West 55 Street.

However, when compass points are used *following* a street name to indicate a section of the city, compass points are abbreviated without periods.

5180 Liberty Street, NE

6. Days and months

Do *not* abbreviate the names of days of the week and months of the year.

Wednesday, April, November, December

ABBREVIATIONS (continued)

7. Measurements

Spell out units of measure, except in technical writing.

> 10 by 20 inches
> an 8-gallon container
> 4 by 8 feet

8. Time

Use the abbreviations a.m. and p.m.—with periods and no space between the letters—with numbers.

> 10 a.m.   8:30 p.m.

When using *o'clock,* eliminate a.m. and p.m.

> seven o'clock in the evening (not 7 p.m. o'clock)

9. Additional punctuation and spacing guidelines

a. Keyboard one space between the initials in a name.

> Mr. R. D. Hamilton

b. Abbreviations consisting of small letters and single initials require a period but no space after the internal periods.

> a.m.   c.o.d.

c. One space should follow an abbreviation within a sentence, unless another mark of punctuation immediately follows.

> The sales staff will attend a meeting at the company headquarters in Washington, D.C., but they will then continue on to the conference in Atlanta.

d. Two spaces should follow an abbreviation at the end of a sentence, as the period that ends the abbreviation also marks the end of the sentence.

> The meeting will begin sharply at 10 a.m.

e. No space should follow an abbreviation that is followed by a question or exclamation mark.

> The Chair will convene the meeting at exactly 10 a.m.!
> Will you be ready for your presentation at 9:30 a.m.?

WORD DIVISION

Although word divisions are not desirable, they are sometimes necessary. Try to avoid word division when possible. The following rules, along with your word processing software hyphenation feature, will provide guidelines to make word division decisions easier.

1. Divide words only between syllables. Use a dictionary to determine the syllables in a word.

    con-sist   tran-script

2. Never divide one-syllable words.

    height   thought

3. Do not separate a one- or two-letter syllable from the beginning or ending of a word.

    a-mount (do not divide)
    seat-ed (do not divide)

4. If the root of a word ends in double letters, divide the word *after* the double letters and before the ending.

    will-ing   fall-ing

    However, if the last letter is doubled when you add the ending, divide the word between the double letters.

    begin-ning   plan-ning   omit-ted

5. When a single-letter syllable occurs in a word, divide *after* the single-letter syllable.

    cata-log   sepa-rate

    When two one-letter syllables occur together within a word, divide between the one-letter syllables.

    anxi-ety   gradu-ation   continu-ation

    When the single-letter syllable *a*, *i*, or *u* is followed by the ending syllable *ble*, *bly*, *cle* or *cal*, divide before the vowel.

    prob-ably   cler-ical   depend-able

WORD DIVISION (continued)

This rule applies only when the vowel is written as a syllable by itself. In the following examples, the vowels *a* and *i* are not single-letter syllables.

possi-ble   dura-ble

6. Divide hypenated words only at the hyphen.

self-confidence   son-in-law

7. Divide compound words between the parts of the word.

check-book   there-fore   business-person

8. Do not divide contractions.

couldn't   doesn't

9. When there is a choice between two or more places to correctly divide a word, enough of the word to be divided should be included on the first line to suggest what the complete word will be.

environ-mental   recom-mend

10. Avoid dividing a surname. Try to avoid separating titles, initials or degrees from a surname.

11. Do not divide figures and abbreviations.

12. Avoid ending more than two consecutive lines with hyphens.

13. Do not divide the first or last lines of a page.

14. Avoid dividing the first or last lines of a paragraph.

15. If an address must be divided, separate the parts of the address as shown below.

468 Mercer - Street (not 468 - Mercer Street)
Garden City, - New York 11530 (not Garden City, New York - 11530)

16. If the parts of the date must be divided, it is preferable to separate the date of the month from the year, rather than the month from the day.

July 1, - 1992 (not July - 1, 1992)

NUMBERS

NUMBERS AS FIGURES

Use commas to separate numbers of four or more digits into thousands, millions, billions, etc.

Do *not* use commas in years, house numbers, telephone numbers, ZIP codes, serial numbers, page numbers and decimal fractions.

    1992   page 1803   222-5478   34267 Main Street

    .78540   New York, NY 10023

GENERAL GUIDELINES

The following suggestions adhere to generally accepted rules for number usage:

1. Write all exact numbers above ten in figures.

> We expect 18 employees to attend the meeting.
> Only three supervisors volunteered for training.

2. Use words to express round and approximate numbers.

> We have over three hundred employees at that location.

3. Use words for any number that begins a sentence. If this is awkward, reword the sentence so that the number does not begin the sentence.

> Twenty-five copies of the report were distributed by the secretary.
>
>   *or*
>
> The secretary distributed 25 copies of the report.

4. Use figures in statistical or tabular material.

5. Use words to express adjective numbers.

> Next year marks the twenty-third anniversary of the company.

NUMBERS (continued)

6. Use words to express age (except when used in technical or scientific material).

    She will be twenty-one next March.

7. Use figures to express terms of discount.

    Payment on the complete order is due 30 days from delivery.

8. Use figures to express page numbers.

    The procedure is described on page 356.

9. Use figures to express percentages, followed by the word *percent* spelled out.

    The advertisement stated that there would be a 30 percent discount after the holiday.

10. Use figures to express quantities and measurements, such as heights, weights, degrees, distances, capacities, market quotations.

    The temperature fell to 22 degrees.
    The office is 18 by 33 feet.

ADJACENT NUMBERS

11. Use a comma to separate adjacent numbers when they are both written in words or both written in numbers.

    If you look at page 218, 15 rules are cited.

12. When two consecutive numbers modify the following noun, use figures for one and words for the other. Use words for the number that can be written with the fewest number of words.

    The reward will consist of 100 twenty-dollar bills.

AMOUNTS OF MONEY

13. Use figures to express all amounts of money. Omit the decimal and zeros in expressing whole dollar amounts.

     $3 $6.75 $4,800 $145.50

14. Amounts of money less than $1 should be expressed in figures combined with the word *cents* unless they are used with related amounts of $1 or over.

    The price of the newspaper increased to 75 cents.
    The fees for copying the items were $4.00, $.55 and $2.85.

15. Use figures and words to express round amounts of money in millions or billions of dollars.

    $3 million $10 billion

16. Repeat the dollar sign before each amount in a series of dollar amounts.

    Rent for office space ranges from $2,500 to $6,000 a month.

17. Use words to express an amount of money at the beginning of a sentence. It may be advisable to reword the sentence so that it does not begin with the amount of money.

    Seventy-five dollars was the quotation he received.
    He received a quotation of $75.

TIME

18. Use figures with a.m., p.m., noon or midnight to express time. The terms *noon* and *midnight* may be used with or without the figure 12.

    8 a.m.   9:30 p.m.   11:35 a.m.   12 noon

19. Use words to express time when used with the word *o'clock.*

    eight o'clock

NUMBERS (continued)

20. Use a colon when expressing hours and minutes. Do not include zeros when the even hour is expressed. Do not use a.m. or p.m. with o'clock.

> 5:30 p.m.   8 a.m.   eight o'clock this morning

ADDRESSES

21. Use figures to express house and building numbers except *one*.

> 56 East 72 Street
> 9078 Broadway
> One Fifth Avenue

22. Use words to express street numbers ten and below. Use figures for street numbers above ten.

> Second Avenue
> West 96 Street

23. ZIP codes are expressed in figures preceded by the two-letter state abbreviation and two blank spaces.

> Williamsburg, VA   23185

TELEPHONE NUMBERS

24. Use figures to express telephone numbers. Use parentheses around the area code, if it is included. If an extension number is included, use commas before and after it.

> 222-7349
> (516) 222-7348
> Please call (516) 222-7348, Ext. 442, when you arrive.

DATES

25. Use cardinal numbers (1, 2, . . . 30) when the day is written after the month. Use ordinal numbers (1st . . . 25th) to express days that stand alone or before the month.

> April 5, 1992
> November 22
> the 5th of April

NUMBERS USED WITH NOUNS

26. Use figures to express numbers used directly with nouns, such as page numbers, model numbers, policy numbers, serial numbers and invoice numbers. The noun (except page) is usually capitalized. It is usually not necessary to include the word *Number* or *No.*

> Policy 11236740
> Model 200
> No. 3546 (noun is not included)

PUNCTUATION

THE PERIOD

Keyboarding Notes: Leave two blank spaces after a period at the end of a sentence. One space follows a period after an abbreviation.

1. Use a period at the end of a sentence that makes a statement or expresses a command.

   > We just returned from the conference.
   > Be sure to include the illustrations in the report.

2. Use a period after a courteous request, even though it may sound like a question.

   > Will you please send the brochures today.

3. Use a period after a condensed statement (elliptical expression), which is usually a word or a phrase used as an answer to a question.

   > Yes. Of course. Not at all.

THE QUESTION MARK

Keyboarding Notes: Leave two spaces after a question mark used at the end of the sentence.

1. Use a question mark at the end of a direct question.

   > Where will the meeting be held?
   > Do you have the sales figures ready?

2. Use a question mark at the end of a short direct question that is added to a statement.

   > You will have the information soon, won't you?

THE EXCLAMATION POINT

Keyboarding Notes: Leave two spaces after an exclamation point.

1. Use an exclamation point after a sentence, a phrase or a single word to show strong feeling or emotion. The exclamation point should be used sparingly in business writing.

> Congratulations on your promotion!

THE DASH

Keyboarding Notes: A dash is created by pressing the hyphen key two times. No space is left before, between or after the hyphens.

1. Use a dash before summarizing words, such as *all, these* or other words that follow and summarize a series.

> Jones, Davis, Carlton, Rose--all were in favor of the new policy.

2. For greater emphasis, use a dash in a sentence with parenthetic expressions containing commas. When the expression occurs within the sentence, use a dash before and after it.

> A number of cities on the east coast--for example, Boston, Charlotte, Richmond, Atlanta--are being considered for the new branch office.

3. In place of other punctuation marks, such as commas, semicolons and colons, use a dash to show greater emphasis. The dash should be used sparingly. Overuse will reduce the emphatic effect.

> Some lucky person--and that could be you--will win the first prize vacation.

PUNCTUATION (continued)

PARENTHESES

Keyboarding Note: No space is left between the parentheses and the data they enclose.

1. Use parentheses to enclose material that is not an integral part of the sentence. The material enclosed within parentheses may be a word, a phrase or a sentence.

   The November sales figures (see page 23) are very disappointing.

Keyboarding Note: There is no period at the end of a sentence within parentheses in a sentence, and the sentence does not begin with a capital letter.

   The committee held a meeting (three members were not present) to review the new policies.

2. Use parentheses to enclose numbers or letters preceding enumerated items.

   Please include (a) name, (b) address, (c) telephone number and (d) social security number.

3. Use parentheses to de-emphasize expressions not essential to the meaning or grammatical completeness of a sentence.

   All of the staff members (including part-time employees) were invited to the holiday party.

QUOTATION MARKS

Keyboarding Notes: Do not leave any blank space between the opening or closing quotation marks and the material they enclose.

Closing quotation marks are placed *after* a period or comma.

Closing quotation marks are placed *before* a semicolon or colon.

Keyboard the question mark after the closing quotation mark if the whole sentence is a question.

> What do you mean by ''acceptable behavior''?

Keyboard the question mark before the closing quotation mark if only the quotation is a question.

> The vice president asked, ''Do you approve of the changes?''

1. Use quotation marks to enclose a statement that consists of the exact words of a speaker or a writer (direct quotation).

   > The president said, ''The company is beginning to move in new directions.''

2. Use quotation marks to enclose titles that represent part of a complete published work—for example, articles, essays, short poems, reports, chapters, lessons, sections, tables, plays, sermons and toasts.

   > Have you read the article called ''New Developments in Desktop Publishing''?

3. Use single quotation marks—keyboard the apostrophe—to enclose a quotation within a quotation.

   > The company manual states clearly, ''All employees must be at work the day 'before and after' a vacation.''

4. Use quotation marks as a symbol for inches and for seconds.

   > The printer will take up 25'' of desk space.
   > It took only 30'' to locate the information.

PUNCUATION (continued)

THE COMMA

Keyboarding Notes: Leave one space after a comma in a sentence. When using a comma in large numbers, no spaces are added.

Use a comma:

1. **In a compound sentence** — When the independent clauses in a compound sentence are joined by a coordinate conjunction (*and, but, or* or *nor*), use a comma before the conjunction unless the clauses are very short.

   We received the reports you submitted, and the committee will review them carefully at the next meeting.

2. **In a series** — When the last member of a series of three or more items is preceded by *and, but, or* or *nor*, commas are used to separate the items in the series. A comma is *not* placed before the conjunction.

   We are considering holding next year's conference in Portland, Seattle or Denver.

   When a series ends with *etc.,* use a comma before and after the expression.

   We have ordered stationery, envelopes, file folders, etc., from the office supply store downtown.

3. **With coordinate adjectives** — When two or more adjectives modify a noun *if* each adjective modifies the noun alone (use the comma if you can substitute the word *and* between the adjectives).

   The new assistant is an efficient, dependable employee.

   If the first adjective modifies the phrase composed of the second adjective and the noun, a comma is not used.

   An alert young woman was hired to do the assignment.

4. **With names in direct address** — Use commas to set off the name of a person who is being addressed directly.

   Thank you, Ms. Mandell, for completing the work so soon.

5. **With parenthetic expressions** — Set off a word, phrase, or clause that interrupts the thought of a sentence and is *not* essential to the meaning or the grammatical completeness of a sentence.

> Our sales figures, however, show an increase in January.
> The employees, I am sure, will be interested in the proposal.
> The salary increases are, in my opinion, not warranted now.

6. **With introductory words or phrases** — Use a comma after words such as *consequently, finally, however, nevertheless, accordingly* when used to introduce a sentence.

> Consequently, we will have to reduce our prices.

Use a comma after an introductory infinitive or participial phrase.

> To reduce our costs, we will have to speed up production time.
> Checking the report, he found a number of errors.

Use a comma when the introductory clause is long (5 or more words).

> In accordance with your letter, we will send the items immediately.

Note: The following introductory expressions are always followed by a comma:

In the meantime,	In other words,
For instance,	For example,
On the other hand,	On the contrary,
In addition,	As a matter of fact,
In any event,	

7. **With an introductory clause** — Use a comma when the main clause is introduced by an introductory adverbial clause beginning with words such as *after, since, if, when, because, until, while.*

> While I was on vacation, I had a lot of time to read.

> If you would like to hear about the new products, we can get together when I am in Los Angeles.

Do *not* use a comma if the adverbial clause *follows* the main clause of the sentence.

> I had a lot of time to read while I was on vacation.

PUNCTUATION (continued)

8. **With a nonrestrictive clause** — Use commas to set off a dependent clause that is not necessary to the meaning of the sentence.

> Ms. Jansen, who has been my assistant for many years, is doing the research for the proposal on new products.

Do *not* use commas if the clause is restrictive (necessary or changes the meaning of the sentence).

> Every person who takes the training course will know how to use the software efficiently.

9. **With appositives** — Use commas to set off a word or group of words that is not essential to the meaning of a preceding noun or pronoun. A comma must be used *before* and *after* the words in apposition.

> The book, *Essentials of Business Writing,* contains valuable writing hints.
>
> The new sales manager, Arnold Lewis, will attend the meeting in my place.

10. **With dates** — Use a comma before and after the year, when it follows the month and day. Use a comma to separate the day of the week from the date. Do not set off the year with commas when using only the month and year.

> He will return the call on Monday, December 10.
> They will hold the conference on May 10, 1992.
> In May 1992 we will attend a conference in Chicago.

11. **With titles, degrees and seniority terms** — Use commas to set off titles and academic degrees following the names of individuals.

> Robert A. Bronner, Ph.D., will address the meeting.
> Please refer your questions to Janet Simon, Esq.

Note: Do not use a comma to set off the terms Sr., Jr., and II after a person's name, unless you know that it is the preference of the person.

> David J. Bell, Sr. is chairperson of the committee.

12. **With Inc. and Ltd.** — Do not use a comma before or after Inc. or Ltd. unless the official name of the firm is written with a comma.

> Business Systems Inc. is a source of many of our supplies.

13. **In addresses** — Use a comma between the city and the state, but do not use a comma between the state name and the ZIP code. When giving an address within a sentence, use a comma after the name of the addressee, the street name, the city name, and the state name (unless followed by a ZIP code).

> Jerry went to Richmond, Virginia, for a meeting.

> The manager sent the information to Susan Garrett, 466 West Main Street, Richmond, Virginia 28226.

14. **In numbers** — Use a comma to separate thousands, millions, etc., in numbers of four or more digits.

> 1,256   199,453,555

Do *not* use commas in numbers that represent years, page numbers, house numbers, room numbers, telephone numbers, serial numbers and ZIP codes.

> 1992   page 1300   Room 7687   Invoice 437869

THE SEMICOLON

Keyboarding Notes: Space once after keyboarding a semicolon.

1. Use a semicolon to separate two independent clauses in a compound sentence when the conjunction is omitted.

> Our office staff can complete the job; they are skilled and understand the procedures.

2. Use a semicolon to separate two independent clauses joined by a conjunctive adverb (*consequently, however, nevertheless, therefore,* etc.).

> We are planning a new schedule soon; however, we do not expect to make many significant changes.

PUNCTUATION (continued)

3. Use a semicolon to separate two independent clauses joined by a conjunction when one—or both—of the clauses contains one or more commas.

> If you compile all of the information immediately, our staff will prepare the sales reports; and each of the sales managers will receive copies in time for the annual meeting.

4. Use a semicolon to separate the items in a series when the items themselves contain commas.

> Our sales offices are located in Seattle, Washington; Des Moines, Iowa; Charlotte, North Carolina; and Richmond, Virginia.

THE COLON

Keyboarding Notes: Leave two blank spaces after the colon, except when expressing time.

1. Use a colon to introduce a listing. The listing usually follows expressions such as *the following, as follows, these.*

> We will need to select the following items for the new office: desks, chairs, files, and tables.

2. Use a colon to introduce a long direct quotation or a formal rule or principle.

> At the annual meeting the president said: "We are looking forward to a profitable year ahead. Our studies appear to indicate that there will be an increasing market for our products. We are, therefore, relying on our sales force to conduct a thorough and enthusiastic sales campaign."

3. Use a colon between the hours and minutes when expressing time in figures.

> The meeting is scheduled to begin at 9:30 a.m.

4. Use a colon after the salutation in a business letter with mixed punctuation.

> Ladies and Gentlemen:
> Dear Mr. Gregory:
> Dear Ms. Garrett:

STATE ABBREVIATIONS

Two letter state abbreviations are authorized by the United States Post Office. These abbreviations are written in capital letters and no periods or spaces are used between the letters.

Alabama	AL		Montana	MT
Alaska	AK		Nebraska	NE
Arizona	AZ		Nevada	NV
Arkansas	AR		New Hampshire	NH
California	CA		New Jersey	NJ
Canal Zone	CZ		New Mexico	NM
Colorado	CO		New York	NY
Connecticut	CT		North Carolina	NC
Delaware	DE		North Dakota	ND
Dist. of Columbia	DC		Ohio	OH
Florida	FL		Oklahoma	OK
Georgia	GA		Oregon	OR
Guam	GU		Pennsylvania	PA
Hawaii	HI		Puerto Rico	PR
Idaho	ID		Rhode Island	RI
Illinois	IL		South Carolina	SC
Indiana	IN		South Dakota	SD
Iowa	IA		Tennessee	TN
Kansas	KS		Texas	TX
Kentucky	KY		Utah	UT
Louisiana	LA		Vermont	VT
Maine	ME		Virgin Islands	VI
Maryland	MD		Virginia	VA
Massachusetts	MA		Washington	WA
Michigan	MI		West Virginia	WV
Minnesota	MN		Wisconsin	WI
Mississippi	MS		Wyoming	WY
Missouri	MO			

PROOFREADER'S MARKS

The following symbols represent standardized marks that are used to simplify the editing and revision processes.

Procedure	Symbol
Capitalize	*Cap* ∩ ≡
Close up space	◯
Delete	ℓ
Insert	∧
Insert comma	⌃
Insert space	#
Insert quotation marks	❝ ❞
Move to the left	⊏
Move to the right	⊐
Lower case	*lc* or /
Single space	*ss*
Double space	*ds*
Quadruple space	*qs*
Let stand (ignore correction)	*stet*
Spell out	*sp*
Begin a paragraph	¶
Transpose	∼
Italic type	_____
Boldface type	∼∼∼∼

TERMINOLOGY

Horizontal Spacing Spacing across the page, from left to right

Vertical Spacing Spacing down the page, from top to bottom

Single Spacing Spacing which leaves no blank lines between the lines of writing. For example:

xxxxxxxxxxxxxxxxxxxxxxxxxxxxxxxxxxxxxxxxxxxxx
xxxxxxxxxxxxxxxxxxxxxxxxxxxxxxxxxxxxxxxxxxxxx

Double Spacing Spacing which leaves one blank line between lines of writing. For example:

xxxxxxxxxxxxxxxxxxxxxxxxxxxxxxxxxxxxxxxxxxxxx

xxxxxxxxxxxxxxxxxxxxxxxxxxxxxxxxxxxxxxxxxxxxx

Quadruple Spacing Spacing which leaves three blank lines between lines of writing. For example:

xxxxxxxxxxxxxxxxxxxxxxxxxxxxxxxxxxxxxxxxxxxxx

xxxxxxxxxxxxxxxxxxxxxxxxxxxxxxxxxxxxxxxxxxxxx

Left Margin Distance from the left edge of the paper to the first character on a line

Right Margin Distance from the last character on a line to the right edge of the page

Top Margin Distance from the top edge of a page to the first printed line

Bottom Margin Distance from the last printed line to the bottom edge of the page

Tab Stop Preset point reached by pressing the tab key, rather than using the space bar repeatedly

NOTES

FOR OTHER FIFTY-MINUTE SELF-STUDY BOOKS
SEE THE BACK OF THIS BOOK.

$$\boxed{\text{NOTES}}$$

FOR OTHER FIFTY-MINUTE SELF-STUDY BOOKS
SEE THE BACK OF THIS BOOK.

$$\boxed{\textbf{NOTES}}$$

NOTES

FOR OTHER FIFTY-MINUTE SELF-STUDY BOOKS
SEE THE BACK OF THIS BOOK.

We hope you enjoyed this book. If so, we have good news for you. This title is part of the best-selling *FIFTY-MINUTE*™ *Series* of books. All *Series* books are similar in size and identical in price. Several are supported with training videos (identified by the symbol ⓥ next to the title).

FIFTY-MINUTE Books and Videos are available from your distributor. A free catalog is available upon request from Crisp Publications, Inc., 1200 Hamilton Court, Menlo Park, California 94025.

FIFTY-MINUTE Series Books & Videos organized by general subject area.

Management Training:

ⓥ	Coaching & Counseling	68-8
	Conducting Training Sessions	193-7
	Delegating for Results	008-6
	Developing Instructional Design	076-0
ⓥ	Effective Meeting Skills	33-5
ⓥ	Empowerment	096-5
	Ethics in Business	69-6
	Goals & Goal Setting	183-X
	Handling the Difficult Employee	179-1
ⓥ	An Honest Day's Work: Motivating Employees	39-4
ⓥ	Increasing Employee Productivity	10-8
ⓥ	Leadership Skills for Women	62-9
	Learning to Lead	43-4
ⓥ	Managing Disagreement Constructively	41-6
ⓥ	Managing for Commitment	099-X
	Managing the Older Work Force	182-1
ⓥ	Managing Organizational Change	80-7
	Managing the Technical Employee	177-5
	Mentoring	123-6
ⓥ	The New Supervisor—Revised	120-1
	Personal Performance Contracts—Revised	12-2
ⓥ	Project Management	75-0
ⓥ	Quality at Work: A Personal Guide to Professional Standards	72-6
	Rate Your Skills As a Manager	101-5
	Recruiting Volunteers: A Guide for Nonprofits	141-4
	Risk Taking	076-9
	Selecting & Working with Consultants	87-4
	Self-Managing Teams	00-0
	Successful Negotiation—Revised	09-2
	Systematic Problem Solving & Decision Making	63-7

Management Training (continued):

(v)	Team Building—Revised	118-X
	Training Managers to Train	43-2
	Training Methods That Work	082-5
	Understanding Organizational Change	71-8
(v)	Working Together in a Multicultural Organization	85-8

Personal Improvement:

(v)	Attitude: Your Most Priceless Possession—Revised	011-6
	Business Etiquette & Professionalism	32-9
	Concentration!	073-6
	The Continuously Improving Self: A Personal Guide to TQM	151-1
(v)	Developing Positive Assertiveness	38-6
	Developing Self-Esteem	66-1
	Finding Your Purpose: A Guide to Personal Fulfillment	072-8
	From Technical Specialist to Supervisor	194-X
	Managing Anger	114-7
	Memory Skills in Business	56-4
	Organizing Your Workspace	125-2
(v)	Personal Time Management	22-X
	Plan Your Work—Work Your Plan!	078-7
	Self-Empowerment	128-7
	Stop Procrastinating: Get to Work!	88-2
	Successful Self-Management	26-2
	The Telephone & Time Management	53-X
	Twelve Steps to Self-Improvement	102-3

Human Resources & Wellness:

	Attacking Absenteeism	042-6
(v)	Balancing Home & Career—Revised	35-3
	Downsizing Without Disaster	081-7
	Effective Performance Appraisals—Revised	11-4
	Effective Recruiting Strategies	127-9
	Employee Benefits with Cost Control	133-3
	Giving & Receiving Criticism	023-X
	Guide to Affirmative Action	54-8
	Guide to OSHA	180-5
	Health Strategies for Working Women	079-5
(v)	High Performance Hiring	088-4
(v)	Job Performance & Chemical Dependency	27-0
(v)	Managing Personal Change	74-2
	Managing Upward: Managing Your Boss	131-7
(v)	Men and Women: Partners at Work	009-4
(v)	Mental Fitness: A Guide to Stress Management	15-7
	New Employee Orientation	46-7
	Office Management: A Guide to Productivity	005-1
	Overcoming Anxiety	29-9
	Personal Counseling	14-9
	Personal Wellness: Achieving Balance for Healthy Living	21-3
	Preventing Job Burnout	23-8

Human Resources & Wellness (continued):

Productivity at the Workstation: Wellness & Fitness at Your Desk   41-8

Professional Excellence for Secretaries   52-1

Quality Interviewing—Revised   13-0

Sexual Harassment in the Workplace   153-8

Stress That Motivates: Self-Talk Secrets for Success   150-3

Wellness in the Workplace   20-5

Winning at Human Relations   86-6

Writing a Human Resources Manual   70-X

(v) Your First Thirty Days in a New Job   003-5

Communications & Creativity:

The Art of Communicating   45-9

(v) Writing Business Proposals & Reports—Revised   25-4

(v) The Business of Listening   34-3

Business Report Writing   122-8

Creative Decision Making   098-1

(v) Creativity in Business   67-X

Dealing Effectively with the Media   116-3

(v) Effective Presentation Skills   24-6

Facilitation Skills   199-6

Fifty One-Minute Tips to Better Communication   071-X

Formatting Letters & Memos on the Microcomputer   130-9

Influencing Others   84-X

(v) Making Humor Work   61-0

Speedreading in Business   78-5

Technical Presentation Skills   55-6

Technical Writing in the Corporate World   004-3

Think on Your Feet   117-1

Visual Aids in Business   77-7

Writing Fitness   35-1

Customer Service/Sales Training:

Beyond Customer Service: The Art of Customer Retention   115-5

(v) Calming Upset Customers   65-3

(v) Customer Satisfaction—Revised   084-1

Effective Sales Management   31-0

Exhibiting at Tradeshows   137-6

Improving Your Company Image   136-8

Managing Quality Customer Service   83-1

Measuring Customer Satisfaction   178-3

Professional Selling   42-4

(v) Quality Customer Service—Revised   95-5

Restaurant Server's Guide—Revised   08-4

Sales Training Basics—Revised   119-8

Telemarketing Basics   60-2

(v) Telephone Courtesy & Customer Service—Revised   064-7

Small Business & Financial Planning:

The Accounting Cycle	146-5
The Basics of Budgeting	134-1
Consulting for Success	006-X
Creative Fund Raising	181-3
Credits & Collections	080-9
Direct Mail Magic	075-2
Financial Analysis: Beyond the Basics	132-5
Financial Planning with Employee Benefits	90-4
Marketing Your Consulting or Professional Services	40-8
Personal Financial Fitness—Revised	89-0
Publicity Power	82-3
Starting Your New Business—Revised	144-9
Understanding Financial Statements	22-1
Writing & Implementing a Marketing Plan	083-3

Adult Literacy & Learning:

Adult Learning Skills	175-9
Basic Business Math	24-8
Becoming an Effective Tutor	28-0
Building Blocks of Business Writing	095-7
Clear Writing	094-9
The College Experience: Your First Thirty Days on Campus	07-8
Easy English	198-8
Going Back to School: An Adult Perspective	142-2
Introduction to Microcomputers: The Least You Should Know	087-6
Language, Customs & Protocol for Foreign Students	097-3
Improve Your Reading	086-8
Returning to Learning: Getting Your G.E.D.	02-7
Study Skills Strategies—Revised	05-X
Vocabulary Improvement	124-4

Career/Retirement & Life Planning:

Career Discovery—Revised	07-6
Developing Strategic Resumes	129-5
Effective Networking	30-2
I Got the Job!—Revised	121-X
Job Search That Works	105-8
Plan B: Protecting Your Career from Change	48-3
Preparing for Your Interview	33-7